PEGGY'S COVE COOKING

{ RECIPES FROM LUNENBURG, MAHONE BAY, CHESTER, SHELBURNE AND OTHER HISTORIC COMMUNITIES ON NOVA SCOTIA'S SOUTH SHORE }

FORMAC PUBLISHING COMPANY LIMITED

Formac Publishing Company Limited recognizes the support of the Province of Nova Scotia through the Department of Communities, Culture and Heritage. We are pleased to work in partnership with the Culture Division to develop and promote our culture resources for all Nova Scotians. We acknowledge the financial support of the Government of Canada through the Canada Book Fund for our publishing activities. We acknowledge the support of the Canada Council for the Arts which last year invested $24.3 million in writing and publishing throughout Canada.

Design by Meghan Collins

Library and Archives Canada Cataloguing in Publication

Peggy's Cove cooking : Recipes from Lunenburg, Mahone Bay, Chester, Shelburne and other historic communities on Nova Scotia's South Shore

Includes index.
ISBN 978-1-4595-0275-8 (bound)

1. Cooking, Canadian--Maritime Provinces style. 2. Cooking-- Nova Scotia--South Shore (Region). 3. Cookbooks. I. Formac Publishing Company

TX715.6.P415 2013   641.59716'2   C2013-903763-2

Formac Publishing Company Limited
5502 Atlantic Street
Halifax, Nova Scotia, Canada
B3H 1G4
www.formac.ca

Printed and bound in China.

CONTENTS

INTRODUCTION

This souvenir collection of classic recipes was gathered from home kitchens and family restaurants in Peggy's Cove, Lunenburg, Mahone Bay, Shelburne and other historic communities along the South Shore. Characteristic of Nova Scotia's best traditional fare, all of these dishes feature fresh local ingredients and simple food-preparation techniques, so they are easy as well as delicious.

Enjoying seasonal harvest from land and sea is a way of life in Nova Scotia, so you will find something here to serve family, friends and neighbours — for any time of year and any meal — whether it's a sunny spring breakfast, a summer picnic on the beach, a harvest celebration in your community hall or a soul-warming winter supper for two.

From basic boiled dinner, chowders, cobblers and grunt to salads, pickles and breads to simply spectacular planked salmon and lobster Newburg, this down-home Down East cookbook lets you treat yourself to a taste of Maritime Canada whatever the season, whoever you're with and wherever you are.

Enjoy!

CHOWDERS

& SOUPS

MARITIME SEAFOOD CHOWDER

Every Maritime cook has a favourite chowder recipe similar to this one. It starts with potatoes, cream and whatever fresh seafood is available, then you might add a little something here or there to make it uniquely yours — or you can keep it simple. This versatile recipe lets you do either, with delicious results every time! Serve this chowder with fresh-baked Bite-size Buttermilk Biscuits (page 66).

1 can (10 oz) baby clams, with juice
8 slices smoked bacon, finely chopped
2 stalks celery, minced
1 onion, finely chopped
1 cup heavy cream (35% mf)
1 cup milk
½ cup dry white wine
2 bay leaves
1 cup grated baking potato
1 teaspoon fresh thyme
1½ pounds fresh seafood (whitefish, lobster or whatever is available), cleaned
   and coarsely chopped
1 can (10 oz) evaporated milk or heavy cream (35% mf)
¼ cup chopped parsley
Salt and pepper to taste

Reserving juice, drain baby clams and set aside. In large heavy pot over medium-high heat, brown bacon, stirring occasionally, until crisp. Discard half of the fat from pan. Add celery, onion and a splash of water, and sauté until vegetables are tender, about 5 minutes. Stir in cream, milk, wine and reserved clam juice until blended. Reduce heat, stir in bay leaves, potato and thyme, and simmer, stirring occasionally, until thickened and potato is tender, about 15 minutes. Stir in reserved clams, seafood, evaporated milk and parsley. Return to a simmer. Remove and discard bay leaves. Season with salt and pepper to taste.

Serves 4 (with seconds).

CREAMY CLAM CHOWDER

Along our sandy shores clams are free for the digging, making them the star ingredient in many Maritime chowder recipes. This version calls for fresh clams, but you might also use a can of whole baby clams (not the larger surf or bar clams, which are too tough). To lower the fat content of this chowder, you can replace the heavy cream with light cream — the soup won't be as rich, but will still serve up wonderful flavour.

½ cup butter
½ cup chopped celery
½ cup chopped onion
3 tablespoons all-purpose flour
2 cups milk
½ cup heavy cream (35% mf) or light cream (10% mf)
2 tablespoons powdered chicken stock base
1 pound clam meat and liquor
1 cup diced cooked potatoes
2 tablespoons chopped pimento
2 tablespoons chopped parsley

In large heavy pot over medium-high heat, melt butter. Sauté celery and onion until tender (do not allow to brown). Whisk in flour to make roux. Stirring constantly, add milk, cream and chicken stock base. Stir in clam meat and liquor, potatoes, pimento and parsley.

Reduce heat to medium and cook, stirring occasionally, until slightly thickened and heated through (do not let boil).

Serves 6 to 8.

LOBSTER BISQUE

Here is a "company's coming" way to savour all the lobster flavour, even from the shells. Let your family try to guess the secret ingredient — maple syrup!

2 pounds cooked lobster bodies and claw shells
½ cup butter
5 cloves garlic, minced
4 bay leaves
4 star anise, toasted
4 whole cloves, toasted
1 small carrot, peeled and chopped
1 small stalk celery, chopped
1 sweet red pepper, chopped
1 red onion, chopped
1 head fennel, chopped
1 tomato, chopped
1 tablespoon white cracked peppercorns
1 tablespoon tomato paste
1 tablespoon maple syrup
1 cup white wine
½ cup brandy
8 cups heavy cream (35% mf)

Remove and discard lobsters' sand sacs from behind eyes. Break bodies and claw shells into bite-size pieces. Set aside.

In large heavy pot over medium-low heat, melt butter. Stir in garlic, bay leaves, star anise, cloves, carrot, celery, red pepper, onion, fennel, tomato and peppercorns. Cover and sweat until vegetables are tender and beginning to colour, about 5 minutes. Stir in reserved lobster bodies and claw shells, tomato paste and maple syrup and cook, uncovered, until all of the liquid has evaporated and mixture begins to stick to pot, about 8 minutes.

Increase heat to medium-high, stir in wine and brandy and cook, scraping up brown bits from bottom and side of pot, until liquid has evaporated. Reduce heat to medium, stir in cream and slowly bring to a simmer (do not let boil).

Remove from heat, let cool to room temperature, then cover and refrigerate for 2 hours to let flavours blend.

Let come to room temperature. Strain through fine-mesh sieve into clean pot (discard solids). Bring to a simmer and gently cook until heated through, about 2 minutes.

Serves 6.

To toast spices: Heat dry heavy skillet over medium heat. Add spices and toast, stirring or shaking frequently, until fragrant, 2 to 5 minutes.

CABBAGE AND APPLE SOUP

Fresh apples and cabbage from local farms shine in this distinctively textured soup that's rich and creamy, with a deep smoky flavour. You can always substitute milk for the cream if you want a lower-fat version.

2 cups chicken stock
2 cups julienned (1-inch lengths) Savoy cabbage
3 cups cubed, cored and peeled apples
1 tablespoon butter
1 large onion, finely chopped
3 slices smoked bacon, chopped
1 tablespoon all-purpose flour
1 cup heavy cream (35% mf)
Pinch nutmeg
Pepper to taste

In large saucepan, bring chicken stock to a boil. Stir in cabbage and cook until slightly softened. With slotted spoon, transfer to bowl and set aside. Set aside saucepan with stock.

In another saucepan, bring 1 cup water to a boil. Reduce heat to medium, stir in apples and cook until just tender. With slotted spoon, transfer ¾ cup of the apples to bowl with cabbage. Cook remaining apples until thickened into sauce. Set aside.

In skillet over medium-low heat, melt butter. Sauté onion and bacon until onion is tender and bacon is crisp. Discard all but 1 tablespoon of the fat from pan. Stir in flour and cook, stirring constantly, for 1 minute. Whisk into stock along with reserved applesauce, cream, nutmeg and pepper. In batches, transfer to blender and process until blended and smooth. Transfer to large pot over medium-low heat, stir in reserved cabbage and apples and cook, stirring occasionally, until heated through (do not let boil).

Serves 4 to 6.

CHEESY VEGETABLE CHOWDER

∽

The chowder tradition is still going strong in the Maritimes. This adaptation — perfect for guests who aren't seafood lovers — reflects contemporary concerns about adding more vegetables to our diets, but still offers the creamy comfort of this classic.

1 tablespoon butter
1 large onion, minced
1 very small cabbage, cored and chopped
1 teaspoon caraway seeds
4 cups vegetable stock
2 large potatoes, peeled and diced
1 carrot, peeled and diced
1 parsnip, peeled and diced
1 small turnip, peeled and diced
1 cup cubed Cheddar cheese
2 cups light cream (20% mf)

In large heavy pot over medium-high heat, melt butter. Sauté onion, cabbage and caraway seeds until onion is translucent and seeds are fragrant. Add stock, then stir in potatoes, carrot, parsnip and turnip. Reduce heat to medium, cover and bring to a boil. Reduce heat to low and simmer, stirring occasionally, until vegetables are tender.

With glass measure, transfer 1 cup soup to blender, add cheese and process until blended and smooth. Pour cream into heatproof bowl. Slowly pour blended mixture into cream, stirring until smooth, then stir into pot. Cook, stirring up from bottom, until heated through (do not let boil).

Serves 6 to 8.

MEAT & CHICKEN

CHICKEN POT PIE

∞

Perhaps the ultimate comfort food, chicken pot pie is perfect for cold winter nights, but that doesn't mean it can't be a year-round treat. If you wish, you can make this in individual servings, using small tart pans. Similar to the British version, the rich filling has meat bound in a well-seasoned sauce — the vegetables are served on the side.

CHICKEN AND STOCK

1 whole chicken (about 3 lbs)
4 sprigs thyme or sage
2 bay leaves
1 onion, coarsely chopped
1 stalk celery, coarsely chopped
1 carrot, coarsely chopped
2 cups unsalted chicken stock

FILLING

¼ cup butter
1 small onion, minced
1 stalk celery, minced
1 clove garlic, minced
¼ cup all-purpose flour
½ teaspoon dried summer savory
¼ cup white wine or sherry
1 teaspoon salt (about)
1 teaspoon pepper (about)
2 tablespoons chopped fresh sage
2 tablespoons chopped Italian parsley

PIE
Pastry for 10-inch Double-Crust Pie
1 large egg, beaten
1 teaspoon rock or sea salt such as fleur de sel

CHICKEN AND STOCK
In large stockpot, combine chicken, thyme, bay leaves, onion, celery, carrot and stock. Add enough cold water to cover chicken and bring to a boil. Reduce heat to low, cover and simmer for 2 hours. Transfer pot to rack and let cool, refrigerate until chilled (immersed in stock, chicken hydrates completely as it cools). Remove and discard solid fat from top. With tongs, remove chicken. With hands, remove and discard all skin and fat, then shred meat into small pieces and set aside. Strain stock through fine-mesh sieve into saucepan (discard solids) and bring to a boil. Reduce heat to medium and cook until reduced to 1½ cups. Let cool.

FILLING
In skillet over medium-high heat, melt butter. Sauté onion, celery and garlic until onion begins to brown, about 15 minutes. Whisk in flour and summer savory to make roux. Whisk in stock, wine, salt and pepper and cook until blended and thickened. Stir in sage, parsley and reserved chicken. Taste and adjust seasoning, if desired. Transfer to bowl, cover and refrigerate for 30 minutes.

PIE
Cut pastry in half. On lightly floured surface, roll out each half into round about ¼-inch thick. With one round, line nonstick 10-inch pie plate. Scrape in filling, heaping in centre. Cover with second pastry round, trimming excess and pressing edges together to seal. Slit 3 steam vents in pastry, brush with egg and sprinkle with salt.

   Bake in 350°F oven until crust is deep brown, about 35 minutes. Slice into wedges.

Serves 6 to 8.

COUNTRY HAM LOAF

Slice this rustic ham loaf and serve it hot for supper, with potatoes and fresh vegetables. If there are any leftovers, top the slices with mustard in sandwiches for a family picnic. Reminiscent of traditional veal or ham pies served in England, this loaf is flavoured with garlic, which grows so well in Nova Scotia. You can purchase ground ham, or grind your own, adding the ground pork as you work, so the meat mixture is well combined.

HAM LOAF MIXTURE

1½ pounds lean ground ham
1½ pounds lean ground pork
2 large eggs, lightly beaten
1 clove garlic, minced
1 cup dry bread crumbs
1 cup milk
¼ cup chopped parsley
Salt and pepper to taste
3 hard-cooked large eggs, shelled

TOPPING

¼ cup packed light brown sugar
2 teaspoons French mustard such as Dijon
1 teaspoon ginger

HAM LOAF MIXTURE

Grease loaf pan. In large bowl, stir together ham and pork until thoroughly combined. Add beaten eggs, garlic, bread crumbs, milk, parsley and salt and pepper to taste. With hands, mix until blended. Spoon half of the ham mixture into prepared pan, smoothing top. Arrange eggs, end to end, along top, then spoon remaining ham mixture firmly around and over eggs, smoothing top.

TOPPING

In small bowl, stir together sugar, mustard and ginger. Spread over meat loaf. Bake in 325°F oven, basting occasionally, for 1½ hours. Transfer to rack and let stand for 5 to 10 minutes before slicing .

ROASTED PORK AND SAUERKRAUT

Strong evidence of Lunenburg County's settlement by German, Swiss and French immigrants is found in its signature food offerings, one of which is sauerkraut. It's the perfect match for Nova Scotia pork, and heritage pig breeds — such as Berkshire — are increasingly popular. Adjust the amounts of the simple ingredients in this dish to suit your table and taste, and serve it with carrots or turnips, and lots of applesauce on the side. If you have leftovers, remove and refrigerate the potatoes separately or they will taste too salty when you reheat this dish.

Boneless pork roast (about 3 lbs)
28 to 32 ounces prepared sauerkraut or 4 cups homemade sauerkraut,
  with liquid
1 cup apple juice
6 to 8 whole medium potatoes

In Dutch oven or heavy pot, place pork. Spoon sauerkraut over and around pork. Add juice and enough water to cover pork. Cover and bring to a boil. Reduce heat and simmer for 1½ hours. Push potatoes into pot around pork, cover and simmer until potatoes are soft and pork is fall-apart tender, at least 2 hours.

Serves 6 to 8.

JIGGS' DINNER

Whether you call it Jiggs' dinner or New England boiled dinner, or use corned beef or smoked pork shoulder, there is nothing fancy about this meal — just good food and plenty of it. Mustard Pickles (page 72) are a great accompaniment. Enjoy!

3 pounds salted beef brisket (corned beef)
2 onions, quartered
2 bay leaves
1 teaspoon dried summer savory
½ teaspoon cracked black peppercorns
2 cups chicken stock (about)
1 small head green cabbage, quartered
1 small turnip, cut in 2-inch dice
4 carrots, cut in 1-inch lengths
4 potatoes, halved

In large stockpot, place brisket. Cover with cold water and let soak, changing water halfway through, for 12 hours or overnight. Drain.

In large stockpot or Dutch oven, combine brisket, onions, bay leaves, summer savory and peppercorns. Add stock and enough cold water to cover brisket and bring to a boil. Reduce heat, cover and simmer for 90 minutes.

Add cabbage, turnip, and enough stock or water, if necessary, to cover brisket and vegetables. Cover and simmer for 10 minutes. Add carrots and potatoes, pushing down into liquid. Cover and simmer until vegetables are soft and brisket is fall-apart tender. With slotted spoon, transfer vegetables to serving platter or bowl. Break brisket into chunks and arrange over vegetables. Ladle some of the broth overtop.

Serves 8.

MEATLOAF WITH TANGY DILL SAUCE

Every good cook needs a great meatloaf recipe! This one offers lots of zesty flavour, especially with the sauce that's served on the side. If you're lucky enough to have leftovers, refrigerating the cooked loaf overnight lets the flavours develop, guaranteeing the best meatloaf sandwiches ever!

SWEDISH-STYLE MEATLOAF

1 cup fresh whole wheat bread crumbs

½ cup large-flake rolled oats

2 large cloves garlic

1 large egg, beaten

1 cup coarsely chopped onions

⅔ cup buttermilk

¾ pound lean ground beef

¾ pound ground chicken or turkey

¼ cup chopped fresh dill

1 tablespoon low-sodium soy sauce

½ teaspoon pepper

½ teaspoon ground allspice

¼ teaspoon nutmeg

¼ teaspoon ginger

SAUCE

1 cup plain fat-free yoghurt

2 tablespoons prepared horseradish

2 tablespoons chopped fresh dill

1 tablespoon low-fat mayonnaise

MEATLOAF

Grease 9 by 5-inch loaf pan. In large bowl, stir together bread crumbs and oats. Set aside.

In blender, process garlic, egg, onions and buttermilk until blended and smooth. Scrape into bread-crumb mixture. Add beef, chicken, dill, soy sauce, pepper, allspice, nutmeg and ginger and, with hands, mix until thoroughly combined. Scrape into prepared pan.

Bake in 425°F oven for 15 minutes. Reduce heat to 350°F and bake until cooked through and shrinking away from pan sides, about 45 minutes.

Transfer to rack and let stand for 10 minutes. before slicing.

SAUCE

In small bowl, whisk together yoghurt, horseradish, dill and mayonnaise until blended and smooth.

Serves 8.

GINGER GARLIC PORK CHOPS

Simply mouth-watering! Ginger, garlic, sherry and soy sauce add an exotic flavour to crumb-coated chops that crisp and brown while they're baking. For an easy dinner, pop a few potatoes and pieces of squash into the oven to bake alongside, then serve with applesauce. Yum!

1 large egg, beaten
2 tablespoons low-sodium soy sauce
1 tablespoon dry sherry
½ teaspoon garlic powder or 1 clove garlic, minced
⅛ teaspoon ginger or ½ teaspoon minced fresh ginger
Pepper
4 tablespoons fine dry bread crumbs
4 lean boneless centre rib pork chops (each 4 oz)

Grease baking sheet. In pie plate, stir together egg, soy sauce, sherry, garlic, ginger and pepper. On sheet of waxed paper, spread bread crumbs. One at a time, dip chops into egg mixture, then roll in bread crumbs, turning to coat all over, and transfer to prepared pan.

Bake in 350°F oven for 30 minutes. Turn and bake until tender and no longer pink in centre, about 20 minutes.

Serves 4.

FISH &
SEAFOOD

STEAMED MUSSELS

Found along the coves and bays of our region, mussel farms harvest one of the most popular foods of the area. Healthy, live mussels should have undamaged, closed shells; if exposed to the air, the shells may gape slightly, but will close when lightly tapped. Before cooking, check, and discard any that are damaged or don't close. Serve these mussels with slices of crusty baguette for mopping up the sauce.

5 pounds fresh mussels
3 cloves garlic, minced
2 Roma tomatoes, finely chopped
1 small carrot, peeled and grated
1 small onion, chopped
1 cup white wine
⅓ cup butter
2 tablespoons chopped parsley
Pepper to taste

Under cold running water, scrub and de-beard mussels, discarding any that are damaged or don't close.

In large heavy pot, combine garlic, tomatoes, carrot, onion, wine, butter, parsley and pepper to taste. Stirring constantly, bring to a boil. Stir in mussels to evenly coat. Reduce heat to medium, cover and let steam until mussels have opened, 5 to 7 minutes (do not overcook). With slotted spoon, transfer mussels (discard any that are closed) to individual serving bowls and ladle sauce overtop.

Serves 4 to 6 as an appetizer, 2 to 3 as an entrée.

SCALLOP BAKE

Some of our favourite recipes — the ones we enjoy over and over — are the most uncomplicated of all. Served with pasta or rice and a salad, this easy-to-prepare seafood casserole makes a simply satisfying meal.

1 pound scallops
6 tablespoons butter, divided
1 cup sliced mushrooms
1 cup chopped sweet green pepper
1 cup chopped celery
½ cup finely chopped onion
¼ cup all-purpose flour
½ teaspoon salt
2 cups milk
½ cup bread crumbs
Grated aged Cheddar or Parmesan cheese

Grease 8-cup baking dish. Cut large scallops in half. In pot of simmering salted water, poach for 1 minute. Drain and set aside.

In large skillet over medium-high heat, melt 2 tablespoons of the butter.

Sauté mushrooms, green pepper, celery and onion until onion is translucent. Set aside.

In large saucepan, melt remaining butter. Whisk in flour and salt. Add milk and cook, whisking constantly, until thickened and bubbling. Fold in scallops and reserved mushroom mixture to coat. Scrape into prepared pan. Sprinkle bread crumbs, then cheese, evenly overtop.

Bake in 350°F oven until browned and bubbling, 25 to 30 minutes.

Serves 4.

CEDAR-PLANKED SALMON

Though wild salmon has disappeared from Atlantic waters, farmed Atlantic salmon delivers this delicious fish to many Maritime menus. You can prepare this in the oven, following the recipe, or grill it outdoors in the summer. To grill it, set one burner to high, then place the planked salmon on the unlit side. The indirect heat will cook the salmon without the wood catching fire. For either the oven or the grill, always use an untreated cedar plank that's slightly larger than the salmon fillet.

Juice of 1 lemon
¼ cup extra-virgin olive oil
1 tablespoon chopped fresh basil
1 teaspoon pepper
½ teaspoon salt
1 salmon fillet (1 to 2 lbs)

Weighing down, if necessary, submerge cedar plank in room-temperature water and let soak for several hours.

In shallow baking dish, stir together lemon juice, oil, basil, pepper and salt. Add salmon, turning to coat all over. Cover, refrigerate and let marinate, turning occasionally, for several hours.

Heat plank in 450°F oven for 5 minutes. Transfer salmon to plank and bake until fish flakes easily with fork, 10 to 12 minutes.

Serves 4 to 6.

SALMON LOAF WITH EGG SAUCE

While our grandmothers may have appreciated the "modern" convenience of tinned fish, you can update this classic comfort food with fresh Atlantic salmon. Accompany it with a fresh green salad and a rice pilaf.

SALMON LOAF

2 green onions, chopped

2 cups cooked fresh salmon, flaked, or tinned salmon, drained, skin and bones discarded

2 cups soft bread crumbs

2 large eggs, beaten

½ cup mayonnaise

¼ cup whole milk

2 tablespoons lemon juice

¾ teaspoon salt

SAUCE

1½ tablespoons butter

1½ tablespoons all-purpose flour

1 cup whole milk, scalded

1 hard-cooked large egg, minced

2 tablespoons chopped parsley

Salt and white pepper to taste

SALMON LOAF

Grease 6-cup loaf pan or Bundt pan. In large bowl, gently stir together green onions, salmon, bread crumbs, eggs, mayonnaise, milk, lemon juice and salt.

Scrape into prepared pan, smoothing top.

Bake in 350°F oven until golden, about 35 minutes. Transfer to rack and let stand for 10 minutes. Unmold loaf and slice.

SAUCE

In saucepan over medium-high heat, melt butter. Whisk in flour and cook, whisking constantly, for 2 minutes. Whisk in milk until blended and bring to a boil. Reduce heat to medium-low and simmer, stirring, until thickened. Fold in egg and parsley. Season with salt and pepper to taste. Spoon over salmon loaf slices to serve.

Serves 4 to 6.

PAN-FRIED HADDOCK WITH SOFT-POACHED EGGS

Incredibly popular in local pubs and home kitchens, this seafood dish gets off to the best start with the freshest fish you can find. It's all about tasting the sea in each bite. The poached-egg yolks — buttery and silky smooth —go well with the crunchy crust of the cooked fish. Serve this with Green Tomato Chow Chow (page 71), and you'll achieve perfection on a plate.

PAN-FRIED HADDOCK

4 slices white sandwich bread
2 large eggs, beaten and seasoned with salt and pepper
½ cup all-purpose flour
4 haddock fillets
¼ cup vegetable oil
½ teaspoon coarse salt such as Kosher or sea salt

SOFT-POACHED EGGS

1 tablespoon white vinegar
4 large eggs
Chopped fresh chives or parsley, for garnish

PAN-FRIED HADDOCK

In food processor, pulse bread until in fine crumbs. Transfer to wide shallow dish. Into second wide shallow dish, pour eggs. In third wide shallow dish, spread flour.

With tip of paring knife, remove and discard any small bones along belly line of fillets. One at a time, roll fillets in flour, dip into eggs, then roll in bread crumbs, turning to coat all over.

In large skillet, heat oil over medium-high heat. Fry fillets, turning halfway through, until golden brown, about 6 minutes. Plate each fillet and sprinkle with salt.

SOFT-POACHED EGGS

In deep skillet, bring water to a simmer (for perfect poaching, water should be 180°F), then stir in vinegar. One at a time, crack eggs on rim of saucer, then gently slide into pan. With wooden spoon, gently roll each egg white over its yolk until eggs start to set and poach until set, 4 to 5 minutes. With slotted spoon, remove each egg from pan, tap back of spoon on paper towel to remove excess moisture, then place egg on fillet and garnish with chives.

Tip: You can poach eggs, immediately transfer and hold in ice-cold water for up to 30 minutes, then reheat in simmering, salted water for 1 minute, before serving.

Serves 4.

FISH AND CHIPS

Fish and chips is easily the most common item on restaurant menus in the Maritimes — and maybe across Canada. While haddock is often used, any fresh fish will work in this recipe. Serving the potatoes cold, like potato chips, makes this dish even easier!

1 pound fresh cod or haddock fillets
½ cup all-purpose flour
1 tablespoon salt, divided
1 teaspoon pepper
2 large eggs
3 tablespoons milk
1 cup fine dry bread crumbs
10 small potatoes, peeled
8 cups canola oil (about)

With paper towel, pat fillets dry. Cut into 2-ounce portions. In shallow dish, stir together flour, 1 teaspoon of the salt and pepper. In second shallow dish, whisk together eggs and milk until blended. In third shallow dish, spread bread crumbs. One at a time, roll fillet portions in flour, dip into egg mixture, then roll in bread crumbs, turning to coat all over, and transfer to platter. Set aside.

With mandoline, slice potatoes as thinly as possible and transfer to colander. Rinse under cold running water, then drain on paper towels and pat dry. Into deep fryer or straight-sided deep wide pot, pour enough oil until no more than one-fifth of the way up side. Heat until deep-fry thermometer registers 300°F. One at a time, carefully drop potato slices into oil and and cook until lightly golden. With slotted spoon, transfer to paper towel–lined bowl. Sprinkle with remaining salt and let drain and cool.

Increase heat. When deep-fry thermometer registers 360°F, carefully drop fillet portions into oil and cook until deep golden brown and bobbing to surface. With slotted spoon, transfer to paper towel–lined plate to drain, then serve hot with reserved chips.

Serves 4 to 6.

LOBSTER ROLLS

Lobster boats dot the waters along Nova Scotia's shores, and lobster rolls dot the tables in almost every small restaurant in the region. For the real down-home experience, bake your own rolls, then serve the filled rolls with fries and creamy coleslaw on the side. The recipe for the rolls will leave you with eight extras, which you can freeze for serving with salad or soup, or make into sandwiches for another meal.

ROLLS

½ cup lukewarm water
⅓ cup granulated sugar, divided
1 tablespoon active dry yeast
1⅓ cups warm water
⅓ cup vegetable oil
1 teaspoon salt
5 to 6 cups all-purpose flour
1 tablespoon butter, melted, for glaze

FILLING

3 cups chopped (bite-size) cooked lobster meat
¼ cup finely chopped celery
Salt and pepper to taste
Mayonnaise
2 cups shredded lettuce

ROLLS

In glass measure, stir together water, 1 teaspoon of the sugar and yeast. Let stand until frothed to at least 1 cup in volume.

In large bowl, whisk together remaining sugar, water, oil and salt. Beat in yeast mixture until smooth. One cup at a time, beat in flour, blending well after each addition, until mixture is thick enough to require wooden spoon and your hands to mix.

On lightly floured surface, knead until smooth and slightly sticky, about 5 minutes. Gather into ball and transfer to greased bowl, turning to coat. Cover and let rise in warm, draft-free place until doubled in volume, about 45 minutes.

Punch down. Divide into 12 same-size pieces, then shape each into oblong roll and transfer to greased baking sheet. Loosely cover with a clean, dry tea towel and let rise for 45 minutes.

Bake in centre of 375°F oven until light golden, 12 to 15 minutes. Transfer to rack, brush tops with butter and let cool. Cut 4 rolls almost in half horizontally and open each on individual serving plate.

FILLING

In bowl, gently stir together lobster, celery, salt and pepper to taste and just enough mayonnaise to bind mixture. Divide evenly among 4 rolls and top with ½ cup of the lettuce.

Serves 4.

LOBSTER NEWBURG

This Lobster Newburg tops the list of favourites on many traditional menus. Spoon it hot into puff-pastry shells, or serve it over rice with a medley of seasonal vegetables.

⅓ cup butter
4 cups chopped (bite-size) fresh lobster meat
½ cup medium-dry sherry
Generous pinch paprika
Generous pinch nutmeg
6 large egg yolks, lightly beaten
2 cups heavy cream (35% mf)

In top of double boiler set over hot (not boiling) water, melt butter. Gently sauté lobster until heated through. Gently stir in sherry, paprika and nutmeg and rewarm.

In bowl, whisk together yolks and cream until blended and smooth. Gently stir into lobster mixture and rewarm, stirring, until thickened and heated through (do not let boil).

Serves 6.

BOILED LOBSTER

No visit to the East Coast is complete without a homestyle feed of lobster! While some big appetites want four- or five-pounders, smaller lobsters, between one and two pounds, might be the most tender. If selecting live lobsters, check that they are active in the tank and have both claws intact; the colour may range from blue to mottled green. Female lobsters are meatier and contain the roe; they are distinguished by their wide abdomens and set of soft swimmerets where their bodies meet their tails. Remove the rubber bands from the claws just before cooking. Don't crowd the kettle; it's better to cook in batches, if necessary.

6 live lobsters (each 1½ lbs)
½ pound butter, melted
2 large lemons, cut in wedges

In large kettle, bring enough water to cover lobsters to a boil, adding 1 tablespoon salt per 1 quart water. Drop live lobsters headfirst into kettle and return to a boil. Cover and cook for 15 minutes, until bright red and legs easily pull away from bodies. Drizzle with butter and serve with lemon wedges.

Serves 6.

HOMESTYLE FISH CAKES

The great thing about this recipe — above and beyond the great taste — is that you can prepare these fish cakes, then freeze them for an instant homestyle meal when unexpected guests arrive on your front porch. If you can't find cod, any fresh white-fleshed fish will work in this dish.

5 ounces fresh cod
3 tablespoons butter, divided
½ cup finely diced onion
½ cup finely diced celery
2 cups mashed potatoes
2 teaspoons salt
1 teaspoon white pepper
1 cup all-purpose flour
2 large eggs, beaten
¼ cup milk
2 cups fine dry bread crumbs

In large saucepan, arrange cod, cover with water and bring to a simmer. Poach until fish flakes easily with fork, 8 to 10 minutes. With slotted spoon, transfer to paper towel–lined platter. Set aside.

In small skillet, melt 1 tablespoon of the butter. Sauté onion and celery until tender. Transfer to large bowl. Stir in cod, potatoes, salt and pepper. Let cool. With hands, shape into patties and transfer to tray or baking sheet.

In bowl, place flour. In second bowl, whisk together eggs and milk. In third bowl, place bread crumbs. One at a time, roll cakes in flour, shake off excess, dip into egg mixture and roll in bread crumbs, turning to coat all over.

In large skillet over medium-high heat, melt remaining butter. Fry cakes, turning once halfway through, until golden brown, about 15 minutes.

Serves 6.

EGGS, CHEESE, BEANS

LOBSTER OMELETTE

Anyone who lived in a lobster-fishing community in the 1950s will tell you that lobster was so plentiful, it was considered a food for poor people. The local children of the day were even embarrassed to take lobster sandwiches — especially when made with homebaked bread — to school in their lunch boxes. Imagine! Served with toast points, this is a great recipe for a brunch crowd.

LOBSTER SAUCE

2 cooked lobsters (each 1 to 1½ lbs)
2 cups heavy cream (35% mf), divided
2 teaspoons cornstarch
12 ounces Swiss cheese, shredded
1 tablespoon fresh tarragon
Salt and pepper to taste

OMELETTES

36 large eggs
¾ cup milk, divided
¼ cup butter, divided

LOBSTER SAUCE

Remove and discard lobster shells (reserve any roe to colour sauce). Chop meat and set aside

In large saucepan, heat 1¾ cups of the cream over medium-high heat. In bowl, whisk together cornstarch and remaining cream until blended and smooth. Stir into pan and bring to a boil. Cook, stirring constantly, until thickened. Reduce heat to low, stir in cheese and cook, stirring, until melted.

Gently stir in reserved lobster, tarragon and salt and pepper to taste and simmer, stirring occasionally, for 15 minutes.

OMELETTES

For each: In bowl, whisk together 3 eggs and 1 tablespoon of the milk. In small omelette pan or non-stick skillet over medium-high heat, melt 1 teaspoon of the butter. Pour in egg mixture. Cook, shaking pan occasionally, until almost set and bottom is light golden. With spatula, fold opposite edges to centre, forming cigar shape, then roll onto warmed plate. Split top lengthwise, then fill with ¼ cup of the sauce.

Serves 12.

CRUSTLESS QUICHE

Quiche is so accommodating. You can add mushrooms or diced cooked broccoli, replace the bacon with ham, omit the onions and throw in whatever cheese you like! Just remember that eggs are delicate, so whisk and cook them gently!

3 tablespoons grated Parmesan cheese, divided
1 tablespoon butter
1 cup chopped onion
½ cup diced cooked bacon (¼ lb)
2 cups shredded Cheddar or Swiss cheese
5 large eggs
1 cup heavy cream (35% mf)
1 cup whole or 2% milk
½ teaspoon salt
½ teaspoon pepper
½ teaspoon paprika

Lightly grease 9-inch pie plate, then sprinkle with half of the Parmesan cheese.

In heavy skillet over medium-high heat, melt butter. Sauté onion until pale golden, about 5 minutes. Stir in bacon. Arrange evenly in plate, then sprinkle with Cheddar cheese.

In large bowl, whisk together eggs, cream, milk, salt and pepper and pour into plate. Sprinkle with paprika and remaining Parmesan cheese. Bake in centre of 400°F oven until golden and set in centre, 25 to 30 minutes. Transfer to rack and let cool completely. Cut into wedges.

Serves 6.

HOMESTYLE BAKED BEANS

It's a good bet that no Maritime meal has been shared more often over the years than Saturday-night baked beans and Oatmeal Brown Bread (page 65). Using your slow cooker keeps it simple, and the big batch cooks up enough for a surprise dinner guest or three!

1 pound dried New Brunswick soldier beans or navy beans
Bouquet garni (1 bay leaf, 2 sprigs celery leaves and 5 sprigs parsley, wrapped in cheesecloth and tied into bundle)
½ pound salt pork, sliced ¼ inch thick
1 onion, chopped
½ cup fancy molasses
¼ cup packed brown sugar
2 teaspoons dry mustard
¼ teaspoon pepper

In large stockpot, place beans and add enough water to cover. Let soak overnight. Drain.

In large stockpot over low heat, combine beans and bouquet garni and add enough water to cover. Cook until beans are tender and bean skin breaks if you blow on it, about 2 hours. Reserving cooking liquid, drain beans and discard bouquet garni. Set cooking liquid aside.

In slow cooker, spread half of the beans over bottom, then arrange half of the pork slices over top. Repeat with remaining beans and pork.

In bowl, stir together 1 cup of the reserved cooking liquid, onion, molasses, sugar, mustard and pepper. Pour into slow cooker. Set on low, cover and cook, stirring halfway through and adding some of the remaining cooking liquid to bring to desired consistency, for 10 hours.

Serves 8.

SALADS &
SIDE DISHES

WARM POTATO SALAD

∞

Here in the Maritimes — with our huge potato harvests from Prince Edward Island and New Brunswick — potato salad is a staple in every cook's repertoire. The tangy hits in this German-inspired salad are the tart cornichon pickles! In a pinch, dill pickles — not sweet — can stand in for the cornichons.

5 unpeeled russet potatoes, scrubbed
5 hard-cooked large eggs, shelled and halved
8 cornichons, finely diced
Small bunch chives, chopped
1 tablespoon Dijon mustard
½ cup vegetable oil
¼ cup white wine vinegar
Salt and pepper to taste

In large pot, place potatoes, add enough cold water to cover and bring to a boil. Reduce heat to medium-high, cover and cook until just fork-tender, about 20 minutes. Drain and let cool enough to handle. Cut into bite-size pieces, return to pot, cover and keep warm.

Remove yolks from eggs and press yolks through fine-mesh sieve into large salad bowl. Set aside. Chop egg whites into bite-size pieces. Gently stir into potatoes along with with cornichons and chives.

Whisk mustard into yolks until blended. Slowly whisk in oil, then vinegar, until blended and smooth. Lightly toss in potato mixture. Serve warm.

Serves 4.

HODGEPODGE

A traditional Maritime summer treat, hodgepodge is a mixture of fresh vegetables, cooked together, then served with cream and butter. This version of the dish comes from the curator of the Fisherman's Life Museum in Jeddore Oyster Pond, Nova Scotia. At the museum, you can see the small home, gardens and outbuildings shared by an inshore fisherman, his wife and their thirteen daughters. The site has been preserved as it was more than a century ago.

1½ cups sliced baby carrots
1½ cups chopped (1 inch lengths) green beans
1½ cups chopped (1 inch lengths) yellow beans
1 onion, diced
1½ cups quartered scrubbed unpeeled tiny new potatoes
1½ cups freshly shelled peas
½ cup half-and-half cream (10% mf)
2 tablespoons butter
White pepper to taste

In large saucepan of unsalted water over medium-high heat, bring carrots and beans to a boil. Reduce heat to medium-low, cover and simmer until tender, about 7 minutes. Stir in onion and potatoes and cook for 10 minutes. Stir in peas and cook for 5 minutes.

Drain all but ¼ cup of water from pan. Gently stir in cream, butter and white pepper to taste.

Serves 4.

COLCANNON

This traditional side dish is a reflection of the Irish heritage of many Nova Scotians, and offers a delicious contrast of textures as well as flavours. It's a great dish for Autumn, when local kale comes into season.

1 teaspoon salt
1½ pounds unpeeled yellow-fleshed potatoes, quartered
8 ounces green kale, coarsely chopped
½ cup butter
¼ cup thinly sliced green-onion tops
1 teaspoon pepper

In pot of boiling salted water, cook potatoes for 12 minutes. Drain, leaving enough water to come halfway up potatoes in pot. Stir in kale. Reduce heat to medium-low, cover and simmer until potatoes are very soft. With colander, drain well. Return potato mixture to pot. Add butter, green-onion tops and pepper. With fork or potato masher, roughly smash until chunky in texture.

Serves 6.

BREADS & ROLLS

BUTTERY GLAZED CINNAMON ROLLS

∞

Many of us have tasted baked goods so fresh, light and moist that we have wondered about the secret of their amazing texture. This homestyle recipe reveals the answer: adding mashed potatoes and their cooking water. These ingredients, a treasured Maritime tradition, enhance the flavour and texture, helping keep bread and biscuits fresh for a longer period. These secret ingredients are a treasured Maritime tradition.

DOUGH

½ cup warm mashed potatoes
½ cup warm potato water
½ cup scalded milk
4 cups all-purpose flour, divided
1 tablespoon (1 package) active dry yeast
½ cup granulated sugar, divided
½ cup butter or margarine, softened
2 large eggs
¾ teaspoon salt
1 tablespoon butter (approximate), melted, to brush on dough while it rises

FILLING

½ cup butter, softened
1 cup packed brown sugar
2 teaspoons cinnamon
Chopped nuts (optional)

GLAZE

1 tablespoon milk
2 teaspoons butter or margarine, melted
¼ teaspoon vanilla extract
⅔ cup icing sugar

DOUGH

In large bowl combine mashed potatoes, water, milk and ½ cup of the flour until blended and smooth. Set aside and let cool to lukewarm.

In glass measure, stir together ¼ cup lukewarm water, yeast and ½ teaspoon of the sugar. Let stand until frothy and doubled in volume, about 10 minutes. Stir into potato mixture. Set aside.

In medium bowl, beat together butter and sugar until light and fluffy. Beat in eggs and salt until blended and smooth. Stir into potato mixture. Stir in remaining flour. Turn out onto lightly floured surface and knead about 100 times, adding more flour if necessary to prevent dough from sticking. Gather into ball and place back in large bowl. Brush with melted butter, cover with clean tea towel and let rise in warm, draft-free place until doubled in volume, about one hour. Punch down. On lightly floured surface, roll out rectangle about 16 x 20 inches.

FILLING

Line large rimmed baking sheet with parchment paper.

With fingertips, spread butter over dough. Sprinkle evenly with brown sugar, cinnamon and, if desired, chopped nuts. Beginning at one long edge, roll up dough over filling jelly-roll style, pressing second long edge to seal. Cut roll into 1-inch slices and transfer, ½ inch apart, to prepared pan. Cover with clean tea towel and let rise until doubled in volume, about 45 minutes. Bake in 375°F oven until browned, 16 to 20 minutes. Transfer to rack to cool.

GLAZE

In small bowl, whisk milk, melted butter, vanilla and icing sugar until smooth and blended. Brush over tops of hot rolls. If glaze is too thick, whisk in a few more drops of milk.

Makes about 2 dozen.

OVERNIGHT ROLLS

Perfect for novice bakers, this no-fail recipe yields dozens of pull-apart buns for family lobster boils, neighbourhood potlucks or charity bake sales. Excellent when fresh, they do dry out quickly, so stock up your freezer with any leftovers.

2 packages active dry yeast
1 teaspoon granulated sugar
4 large eggs
¾ cup granulated sugar
½ cup vegetable oil
2 teaspoons salt
10 cups all-purpose flour
Shortening, for glaze

Grease baking sheets. In glass measure, stir together ½ cup warm water, yeast and 1 teaspoon sugar. Let stand until frothy, about 10 minutes. In large bowl, beat eggs. Stir in 2½ cups warm water, ¾ cup sugar, oil and salt until blended and smooth. Stir in yeast mixture and flour. On lightly floured surface, knead until smooth and elastic, 5 to 10 minutes, Gather into ball, cover with clean tea towel and let rise in warm, draft-free place for 2 hours. Punch down, cover and let rise for 1 hour. With hands, shape into 2-inch-diameter buns and transfer to prepared pans (buns should fit snugly side by side). Cover and let rise overnight.

Bake in centre of 375°F oven for 10 minutes. Transfer to racks. Lightly brush tops of hot buns with shortening. Let cool.

Makes 6 dozen.

OATMEAL BROWN BREAD

A true Maritime tradition, this recipe makes two loaves laced with molasses, which round out any hearty meal. Homestyle Baked Beans (page 53) aren't complete without this wonderful bread on the side.

1 cup large-flake rolled oats
½ cup fancy molasses
2 tablespoons lard
2 teaspoons salt
1 teaspoon fancy molasses
1 package active dry yeast
5 cups all-purpose flour

Grease two 9 by 5-inch loaf pans. In large heatproof bowl, stir together oats, ½ cup molasses, lard and salt. Stir in 2 cups boiling water until lard has dissolved. Let cool to lukewarm.

In glass measure, stir together ½ cup lukewarm water, 1 teaspoon molasses and yeast. Let stand until frothy and doubled in volume. Stir into oat mixture. One cup at a time, stir in flour until combined.

On lightly floured surface, knead dough until smooth, 4 to 5 minutes. Gather into ball and transfer to lightly greased bowl, turning to coat. Cover with clean tea towel and let rise in warm, draft-free place until doubled in volume, about 1 hour.

Punch down, divide in half and shape into 2 loaves. Place each in prepared pan. Cover and let rise for about 1 hour.

Bake in centre of 350°F oven for 30 to 40 minutes. Remove from pans and transfer to racks. Let cool.

Makes 2 loaves.

BITE-SIZE BUTTERMILK BISCUITS

These friendly little biscuits are delicious served with soup, salad or an entrée. By adding fresh herbs to the batter, warm biscuits make the perfect base for savoury appetizers. In addition, you can also use them (without the chives) in a sweet dessert, such as strawberry shortcake.

2 cups all-purpose flour
1 tablespoon baking powder
2 teaspoons granulated sugar
¼ teaspoon salt
½ cup cold butter, cubed
1 large egg
1 cup buttermilk
¼ cup chopped fresh chives (optional)

Lightly grease 2 rimless baking sheets. In large bowl, whisk together flour, baking powder, sugar and salt. With pastry blender or two knives, cut in butter until mixture resembles coarse crumbs. In another bowl, whisk together egg and buttermilk until blended. Stir in chives, if desired. With fork, stir into flour mixture until soft dough forms.

   On lightly floured surface, gently knead 2 or 3 times. Drop by tablespoons onto prepared pans. Bake in 400°F oven until golden, about 15 minutes (for large biscuits, roll out dough 1 inch thick, cut with 2-inch biscuit cutter and bake in 400°F oven for 30 to 35 minutes).

Makes 36 bite-size or 10 large biscuits.

SOLOMON GUNDY

In Nova Scotia, pickled herring aren't hidden in a jar at the back of the fridge. Many German immigrants who came to the South Shore community of Blue Rocks in Lunenburg County brought their recipes for "salmagundi." Here's a simple version of this down-home Down East delicacy, rechristened Solomon Gundy or Solomon Grundy.

6 salt herring
2 onions, sliced
2 cups vinegar
½ cup granulated sugar
2 tablespoons mixed pickling spice

Remove and discard herring heads and tails. Clean insides and remove and discard skins. Cut into pieces about 1 inch thick, then fillet pieces. Transfer to bowl, cover with cold water and let soak for about 24 hours. Squeezing out water, transfer pieces to wide-mouth 500 mL preserving jar, alternating herring layers with onions.

In saucepan, bring vinegar, sugar and pickling spice to a boil. Immediately remove from heat and let cool. Pour into jar. Cover and refrigerate for 4 to 6 days.

Makes 1 500 mL jar.

GREEN TOMATO CHOW CHOW

A familiar companion of boiled potatoes in Atlantic Canada, traditional Chow Chow is a tangy condiment that complements fall and winter fare. And it's the perfect use for an overflowing harvest of homegrown green tomatoes picked after the first frost.

5 quarts green tomatoes, thinly sliced
6 large onions, thinly sliced
⅓ cup coarse pickling salt
6 cups granulated sugar
4 cups white or cider vinegar
¼ cup mixed pickling spice, wrapped in cheesecloth and tied into bundle

In large glass bowl, stir together tomatoes, onions and salt to coat. Cover and let stand overnight. Transfer to colander and thoroughly rinse under cold running water, then press out excess moisture.

In large heavy pot, bring sugar and vinegar to a boil. Add pickling-spice bundle and tomato mixture. Reduce heat to low and simmer, stirring often, until thickened and vegetables are tender, about 1½ hours. Ladle into hot sterilized preserving jars, leaving ½-inch headspace. Seal and process for 10 minutes.

Makes 12 cups.

MUSTARD PICKLES

Every family in the Maritimes has its favourite version of mustard pickles. This recipe makes a thick and smooth chutney-style pickle. It's a great garnish spooned over fish, meatloaf, burgers or sausages.

4 stalks celery, minced
10 cups diced ½ inch unpeeled English cucumbers
5 cups diced onions
1 cup minced sweet red pepper
1 cup minced sweet green pepper
¾ cup rock salt
8 cups granulated sugar
6 cups white vinegar
4 tablespoons dry mustard
4 tablespoons turmeric
3 tablespoons whole yellow mustard seeds
2 tablespoons pepper
1 tablespoon crushed fenugreek
1 tablespoon cumin
1 cup cornstarch

In large heatproof bowl, stir together celery, cucumbers, onions, and red and green peppers. In large pot, bring 5 cups water and salt to a boil. Pour over celery mixture and let stand for 2 hours. Drain and set aside.

In large stockpot, stir together sugar, vinegar, mustard, turmeric, mustard seeds, pepper, fenugreek and cumin until thoroughly mixed and sugar has dissolved. Remove 2 cups and set aside.

Stir celery mixture into stockpot and bring to a boil. Reduce heat to medium and cook until thickened, at least 15 minutes. Stir cornstarch into reserved sugar mixture. Stir into stockpot. Increase heat to high and, stirring occasionally, return to a boil. Cook, stirring constantly, until thickened. Reduce heat and simmer for 3 minutes. Ladle into hot sterilized preserving jars, leaving ½-inch headspace. Seal and process.

Makes 7 to 8 quarts.

DESSERTS

APPLE CRISP

∞

Could there be any easier dessert than a crisp? You can bump up the quantities to make more for a large crowd, and replace the apples with any seasonal fruit. If you use spring rhubarb, add extra sugar to cut the tartness; with summer peaches, add slightly less. Fresh-picked blueberries are simply fabulous, and, in the fall, you can't go wrong with Gravenstein, Jonagold or McIntosh apples.

8 cups thinly sliced cored peeled apples
½ cup granulated sugar
2 tablespoons lemon juice
1 cup packed brown sugar
1 cup all-purpose flour
1½ teaspoons cinnamon
¼ teaspoon nutmeg
1½ cups large-flake rolled oats
¾ cup butter, cubed and brought to room temperature
Vanilla ice cream

Grease 9 by 13-inch baking dish. In large bowl, toss together apples, granulated sugar and lemon juice. Spread evenly in prepared pan. In small bowl, with fingertips, combine brown sugar, flour, cinnamon and nutmeg. Toss in rolled oats, then butter, until combined and crumbly. Sprinkle evenly over apple mixture.

Bake in centre of 375°F oven until top is golden and filling is soft and bubbling, about 40 minutes. Serve warm with ice cream.

Serves 10.

BLUEBERRY GRUNT

Blueberry Grunt is a homey dessert with a whimsical name that belies its serious good taste. Serve it warm, topped with vanilla ice cream or whipped cream.

SAUCE

2 cups fresh or frozen blueberries
¼ to ½ cup granulated sugar

DUMPLINGS

1 cup all-purpose flour
2 teaspoons baking powder
1 teaspoon granulated sugar
¼ teaspoon salt
1 tablespoon cold butter
⅓ to ½ cup milk

SAUCE

In large saucepan, stir together blueberries, sugar and 1/3 cup water and bring to a boil. Reduce heat and simmer, stirring occasionally, until thickened and berries have softened, about 5 minutes.

DUMPLINGS

In bowl, whisk together flour, baking powder, sugar and salt. With pastry blender or two knives, cut in butter until mixture resembles coarse crumbs. Stir in just enough milk to form soft dough. Drop by spoonfuls into simmering sauce. Immediately cover and cook, without removing cover, for 15 to 18 minutes. Serve warm.

Serves 4 to 6.

STRAWBERRY RHUBARB PIE

∞

A match made in early-summer heaven, the combination of strawberries and rhubarb serves up a sweet harvest from local farms — and kitchens!

Pastry for 9-inch Double-Crust Pie

1 cup granulated sugar
3 tablespoons all-purpose flour
Generous pinch nutmeg
3 cups chopped rhubarb
1 cup halved, hulled strawberries
1 tablespoon butter, melted

Halve pastry. On lightly floured surface, roll out one half and line 9-inch pie plate. In large bowl, whisk together sugar, flour and nutmeg. Toss in rhubarb and strawberries to coat. Spoon into pie shell. Roll out remaining pastry and place overtop, pressing edges together to seal. Slit 3 or 4 steam vents in top crust, then brush with melted butter.

   Bake in 350°F oven until crust is golden and filling is tender and bubbling, 45 to 60 minutes.

Serves 6 to 8.

CARROT CAKE

This recipe is a winner, and that's been proven by the many bakers who have earned prizes — and countless compliments — for this cake at county fairs. In an airtight container, the icing will keep for up to three weeks in the fridge.

CARROT CAKE

2 cups all-purpose flour
1½ cups granulated sugar
2 teaspoons each cinnamon and baking soda
½ teaspoon each salt, ginger, nutmeg and mace
3 large eggs
¾ cup mayonnaise
2 cups grated carrots
1 cup crushed pineapple, with juice
1 cup raisins
¾ cup chopped walnuts

CREAM CHEESE ICING

1 package (8 oz) cream cheese, softened
2 cups icing sugar
¼ cup butter, softened
1 tablespoon milk

CARROT CAKE

Grease 9 by 13-inch baking pan. In large bowl, whisk together flour, sugar, cinnamon, baking soda, salt, ginger, nutmeg and mace. In another bowl, whisk eggs until blended, then whisk in mayonnaise. Pour into flour mixture. Top with carrots, pineapple and juice, raisins and walnuts and beat until thoroughly mixed. Scrape into prepared pan.

Bake in centre of 350°F oven until springy on top, 35 to 45 minutes.

Transfer to rack and let cool.

CREAM CHEESE ICING

In bowl, beat together cream cheese, icing sugar, butter and milk until light
and fluffy. Ice cooled cake.

Serves 12.

JELLY ROLL WITH LEMON FILLING

Family and friends will love this classic, light and lemony sponge cake that's perfect for a summer picnic.

ROULADE SPONGE

¼ cup all-purpose flour
1 tablespoon cornstarch
4 large egg whites
⅓ cup granulated sugar, divided
8 large egg yolks
Zest of ½ lemon
Pinch salt

FILLING

3 large egg yolks
Zest of 1 lemon
Juice of 2 lemons
½ cup granulated sugar
½ cup white wine
1 envelope (1 tbsp) unflavoured gelatin powder
½ cup heavy cream (35% mf), whipped

Icing sugar and raspberry purée, for garnish

ROULADE SPONGE

Line 12 by 16-inch baking sheet with parchment paper, then spray with baking spray. In small bowl, whisk together flour and cornstarch. Set aside. In second small bowl, beat together egg whites and ¼ cup of the sugar, until soft peaks form. Set aside.

In large bowl, stir together egg yolks, remaining sugar, zest and salt. One-third at a time, gently fold egg whites into yolk mixture. Sift flour mixture overtop, then gently fold in until just combined. Pour into prepared pan, smoothing top.

Bake in centre of 425°F oven until sponge springs back when lightly touched, 7 to 10 minutes. Turn out onto clean, damp tea towel. Beginning at one long edge, roll up. Set aside.

FILLING

In large heatproof bowl over saucepan of simmering water, whisk together yolks, zest, juice, sugar and wine until light and fluffy and thermometer inserted in mixture registers about 110°F. Stir in gelatin, remove from heat and let stand until dissolved.

Place bowl over bowl of ice and water and whisk until just cooled (do not allow gelatin to set). Gently fold in whipped cream.

Unroll sponge. Leaving 1-inch border along edges, evenly spread with filling.

Beginning at one long edge, reroll sponge around filling, lifting corresponding edge of towel and pulling upward to roll. Transfer roll, seam side down, to platter or tray, cover and refrigerate for 40 minutes.

Dust with icing sugar and slice. Place each slice on individual serving plate, add spoonful of raspberry purée alongside.

Serves 12.

GINGERBREAD WITH BLUEBERRY SAUCE

This time-honoured treat is part of Nova Scotia's Scottish heritage. Delicious on its own, the gingerbread dresses up for company, topped with either the blueberry sauce or lemon curd (you can make the lemon curd in advance; it keeps for up to two weeks in the fridge). For an elegant finish, spoon the warm sauce over the cake, then add a generous dollop of whipped cream flavoured with a dash of coffee brandy.

GINGERBREAD

2½ cups all-purpose flour
1 teaspoon each ginger, cinnamon and ground cloves
½ teaspoon salt
¾ cup granulated sugar
½ cup shortening
1 large egg
1 cup fancy molasses
1½ teaspoons baking soda

BLUEBERRY SAUCE

2 cups fresh or frozen blueberries
¾ cup granulated sugar
1 teaspoon lemon juice

LEMON CURD

2 large eggs
2 large egg yolks
½ cup granulated sugar
Zest of 2 lemons, minced
½ cup lemon juice
Pinch salt
6 tablespoons unsalted butter, cubed

GINGERBREAD

Grease 8 by 12-inch baking pan. In bowl, mix together flour, ginger, salt, cinnamon and cloves. Set aside. In large bowl, beat together sugar and shortening. Beat in egg until blended. Beat in molasses until blended. Stir baking soda into 1 cup boiling water until dissolved, then slowly add to sugar mixture, beating until blended. Slowly add reserved flour mixture, beating until blended and smooth. Scrape into prepared pan.

Bake in centre of 375°F oven until toothpick inserted in centre comes out clean, 30 to 45 minutes.

BLUEBERRY SAUCE

In saucepan over medium heat, stir together blueberries, sugar and lemon juice and cook, stirring, until thickened (do not let burn).

LEMON CURD

In heatproof bowl, beat together eggs, egg yolks, sugar and zest until smooth and pale yellow. Beat in juice and salt until blended and smooth. In large pot, bring about 1 quart water to a boil. Reduce heat to a simmer. Set bowl on saucepan rim (bottom of bowl should sit above, not touch, simmering water) and cook egg mixture, stirring constantly with spoon, until thick enough to coat back of spoon, about 20 minutes. Remove from heat. One cube at a time, stir in butter, blending after each addition. Place plastic wrap against surface (to prevent formation of skin) and refrigerate until cooled.

Serves 24.

COOKIES & SQUARES

RHUBARB COCONUT SQUARES

The tartness of the rhubarb sharpens the flavour of these oh-so-sweet squares.

BASE

1 ⅓ cups all-purpose flour
½ cup granulated sugar
Zest of ½ orange
½ cup cold unsalted butter, cubed

FILLING

2 cups diced rhubarb
¼ cup granulated sugar (about)
Juice of 1 orange
2 tablespoons butter
Pinch nutmeg

TOPPING

2 large eggs
Zest of ½ orange
¾ cup granulated sugar
1½ teaspoons vanilla extract
2½ cups shredded unsweetened coconut
2 tablespoons all-purpose flour

BASE

Grease 9-inch square baking pan. In bowl, whisk together flour, sugar and zest. With pastry blender or two knives, cut in butter until mixture resembles coarse meal. Firmly and evenly press into bottom of prepared pan.

FILLING

In saucepan, stir together rhubarb, sugar and juice and bring to a boil. Cook, stirring, until thickened. Stir in more sugar to taste, if desired. Remove from heat. Stir in butter and nutmeg until blended and smooth. Let cool slightly. Evenly spread over base.

TOPPING

In bowl, beat together eggs, zest, sugar and vanilla. Stir in coconut and flour until combined. Evenly spread over filling. Bake in centre of 350°F oven until lightly browned, 25 to 30 minutes. Transfer to rack and let cool before slicing.

Makes 24 squares.

BAKE SALE COOKIES

This big-batch recipe makes 100 cookies — enough for a bake sale, block party or Canada Day celebration. Of course, these cookies are so scrumptious, you may want to just bake them up, pop them into the freezer and pull them out when you need a snack or when family and friends come for a visit.

1 large egg
3½ cups all-purpose flour
1 cup granulated sugar
1 cup packed brown sugar
1 cup butter, softened, or margarine
1 cup vegetable oil
1 teaspoon salt
1 teaspoon cream of tartar
1 teaspoon baking soda
1 teaspoon vanilla extract
1 cup Rice Krispies
1 cup shredded unsweetened coconut
1 cup large-flake rolled oats

In large bowl, beat together egg, flour, sugar, brown sugar, butter, oil, salt, cream of tartar, baking soda and vanilla. Stir in Rice Krispies, coconut and oats until combined. On lightly floured surface, roll out dough about ½ inch thick and cut into cookies. Bake in 350°F oven until golden, 7 to 10 minutes.

Makes 100 cookies.

OLD-FASHIONED OATCAKES

As wholesome and nutritious but a little sweeter than Scottish oatcakes, this version is delicious for breakfast, lunch or a bedtime snack. The recipe makes enough to feed a gathering of the clans, but these oatcakes freeze well, so baking just one batch means you'll have lots on hand for any event.

3 cups large-flake rolled oats
2 cups all-purpose flour
1 cup whole wheat flour
½ cup granulated sugar
½ cup packed brown sugar
1 teaspoon fine sea salt
1 teaspoon baking soda
1½ cups cold unsalted butter, cubed
⅓ cup water (about)
Extra large-flake rolled oats, for rolling

Line baking sheets with parchment paper. In large bowl, stir together oats, all-purpose and whole wheat flours, sugar, brown sugar, salt and baking soda. With pastry blender or two knives, cut in butter until mixture resembles coarse crumbs. Slowly add just enough water to form dough. Scatter extra oats on work surface, place dough on top and sprinkle with extra oats. Roll out to ¼-inch thickness. With knife, cut into 2 by 4-inch cakes and transfer to prepared pans.

Bake in 350°F oven until bottoms are browned, 15 to 20 minutes.

Makes about 96 oatcakes.

SUGAR COOKIES

Sugar cookies are the universal sweet treat — the perfect first baking project for children and just right for tea parties on the lawn. Budding bakers can decorate their cookies with granulated sugars, edible glitter and tiny candies to create one-of-a-kind mini-masterpieces!

1 cup butter, softened
¾ cup granulated sugar
¼ cup packed brown sugar
1 large egg
1 teaspoon vanilla extract
2 cups all-purpose flour
2 teaspoons cream of tartar
1 teaspoon baking soda
¼ teaspoon salt
¼ teaspoon nutmeg
Granulated sugar, for sprinkling
Glazed cherries, quartered, for garnish (optional)

Line baking sheets with parchment paper. In bowl, beat together butter, sugar and brown sugar until creamy and smooth. Beat in egg and vanilla. In another bowl, whisk together flour, cream of tartar, baking soda, salt and nutmeg. Stir into butter mixture until blended. Divide into 4 discs, wrap and refrigerate until chilled. On lightly floured surface, roll out each disc about ¼–½ inch thick and, with cutter, cut out cookies and transfer to prepared pans. Sprinkle with sugar and, if desired, garnish each with cherry quarter. Bake in 375°F oven until golden, 8 to 10 minutes.

Makes about 36 cookies.

SOFT MOLASSES COOKIES

Maritime kitchen tables often had a jar of molasses set beside the salt and pepper shakers. Bread and molasses, pancakes and molasses, and gingersnaps, gingerbread and cookies made with molasses, were familiar and popular traditional fare. These soft molasses cookies dotted with sticky raisins are just as good as ever — and destined to be contemporary favourites, too.

1 large egg
1 cup packed brown sugar
1 cup molasses
1 cup melted shortening
¼ cup hot water
4 teaspoons baking soda
4½ cups all-purpose flour
1 teaspoon cream of tartar
¾ teaspoon salt
Seedless raisins (optional)

Grease baking sheets. In large bowl, beat egg until blended. Beat in brown sugar, molasses and shortening. Stir baking soda into ¼ cup hot water until dissolved, then stir into sugar mixture until blended. Sift flour, cream of tartar and salt over egg mixture and stir until blended. With floured hands, shape dough into 1-tablespoon balls and transfer to prepared pans. Slightly flatten, then, if desired, press raisin into centre of each.

Bake in 350°F oven until lightly browned, 10 to 12 minutes.

Makes 24 to 36 cookies.

INDEX